How to Get the Best Deal Every Time You Travel

By

Lee Harrison & *IL* Editors

www.InternationalLiving.com

How to Get the Best Deal Every Time You Travel
By *International Living*

First published 2005
Second edition 2006

First written by: Lee Harrison
Updated by: Donna Garvin
Editor: Emily Furlong
Graphic design: Ray Holland, Donna Garvin

Cover photography rights: istockphoto.com

ISBN 978-1-905720-00-2

120R0079B5

Table of Contents

Introduction

A new era in travel reservations

L et's face it: the good old days—when you relaxed in your local travel agency reading a magazine while your agent scoured his or her resources for the best deals available, are all but gone. For the most part, and largely through choice, today's travelers are left to their own devices. Unless you're regularly trawling for deals, the number of resources at your disposal—particularly those online—can be overwhelming.

The Internet is a great source of information, but I think everyone has discovered at some point just how much time it's possible to spend online before they find the particular information they're looking for. Sometimes you'll come across people who just seem to be in the know when it comes to good deals and opportunities—but armed with the right information, you too will know where to start looking, and you too will be on the "inside track," and be in the know.

On any given flight, the passengers around you—those sitting in the same section of the airplane—will have paid different fares. Why? Well, it depends on a number of variables…when and where they bought their tickets, the day of the week and month of the year they chose to fly, and how they planned their route.

There was a time when an understanding of the ticketing process, the tariffs, and the industry's pricing practices, was key to getting the best deal on airfares, but not any more. Each airline now seems to have a different tariff system.

Today, you've got to know how, and whom, to ask for the cheapest fare, and you've got to be able to understand the price you're quoted.

Suppose you want to fly from New York City to London—a straightforward and common enough flight. Call an airline that flies that route and ask for the round-trip, economy-class fare. You'll be quoted a rate of, say, $800. Thank the airline representative for his time and hang up. He's done his job. He's given you a starting point—a touchstone to use to compare prices. Now, your work begins.

It's possible to whittle that $800 fare down to $600, even $550. Interested? Of course you are. Read on.

Wishing you many great deals,

Kathleen Peddicord
Publisher, *International Living*

Chapter 1

Plan ahead

The most important thing to remember with any travel booking, is that flexibility means savings. If you can move your travel dates, departure times, and itinerary, there will be a lot more fares open to you. Before you even begin to look for a fare or make a reservation, there are a few things that you should keep in mind.

- **Make your plans as early as possible:** If you can make reservations up to three months in advance, some airlines offer early-bird discounts. Rather than the last-minute specials offered by many airlines, buying tickets earlier is usually better.

- **Be as flexible as possible:** If you are willing to fly with any airline, on any day, at any time, you are much more likely to get a bargain fare. If you are also in a position to be flexible about your departure and destination cities, the price of your airfare can drop even lower.

- **Consider flying to an alternate airport:** You can get cheaper flights by flying to secondary or tertiary airports. Initially, many of the low-cost airlines were using these airports, and now the bigger competitors are beginning to move in and match their fares. For example, if you're going to Manhattan, the airport in Newark, New Jersey is actually closer to downtown than New York's JFK airport...but it's often much cheaper to fly to Newark. **Travelocity.com** now gives you the option of picking more than one airport in an area to compare for the lowest prices. (This feature is currently available for U.S. and Canada searches only.)

- **Pick the off-season:** Knowing the time of year that is considered off-season at your destination can save you money—not only on airfares, but on hotels, cars, and just about everything else. The obvious added bonus is that there'll be fewer crowds to contend with, and you'll get more of a feel for your destination's real personality. Here are the off-season times for various regions of the world:

  > **Europe:** November through March
  > **Asia:** January and February
  > **Australia and New Zealand:** April through August
  > **The Caribbean:** March through November
  > **South America:** April through November

- **Travel on a holiday:** If it's possible, arrange your trip on a holiday, such as Christmas or Thanksgiving Day. You'll find better rates, and often fewer crowds at the airport.

- **Get a feel for the fare beforehand:** Have an idea of what you think the fare should cost before you call the airline or your travel agent. Spend a few minutes checking ads in travel publications and newspapers with travel sections, and surfing the Internet.

- **Check foreign newspapers:** The travel sections of foreign—particularly British—newspapers advertise discount fares to just about anywhere in the world. Why is this important? Consider this example: Almost every major airline that goes to Europe from the U.S. also flies to London. If you want to go to, say, Rome, you can often find deeply discounted tickets in the London papers, offering flights both to the U.S. and to Rome. In the end, you'll sometimes find it hundreds of dollars cheaper to fly via London rather than directly from the U.S. If you don't have a news outlet or library nearby where you can check foreign papers, most of the world's papers have an online version. See *www.telegraph.co.uk* for a good example...although the print copy you'll find at the local library typically has better deals.

• **Consider a "vacation"**: As you know, the highest fares are paid by those last-minute travelers who are no longer in any position to bargain. But here's a tip from Rudy Maxa, the Savvy Traveler, and contributing editor with *National Geographic Traveler Magazine,* that may help: Try contacting the vacation branch of the various airlines. For example, if you have to go to San Francisco at the last minute and find the airfare exorbitant, ask the airline if they have any vacation packages to San Francisco. You may find an excellent airfare and a good hotel rate all in one, and without the advance purchase requirement.[1]

By considering these items ahead of time, you'll have a feel for the degree of flexibility that you're willing to exercise when buying your ticket. You're now ready to do some serious price shopping.

A word about your travel agent

One reader recently wrote, "I've got a local travel agent who's still in business, and I've been doing business with him for years. Could he be getting me the best possible deals?" The short answer is yes, he could be. Although thousands of travel agents have been forced out of business, there are still many good independent agents around. (In this sense, an "independent" agent is one who has no incentive to recommend a particular airline.)

According to author Edward Hasbrouck, "In an effort to deprive the public of the independent advice of travel agents who might recommend their competitors, U.S. airlines have so reduced the commissions they pay travel agents for issuing U.S. and Canada tickets, that most agencies have found it necessary to charge fees for this service. Are travel agents' services worth paying for? Surveys by journalists and consumer organizations have consistently found that good travel agents can use

---

1 Courtesy of Minnesota Public Radio, 2003: *www.mpr.org.* The Savvy Traveler® website, including free recordings of previously aired broadcasts, can be found at: *www.savvytraveler.org.*

their expertise in finding the best fares to save most travelers enough money to cover the agents' fees."[2]

So if you've got an independent travel agent who has won your trust, he or she may be your best resource. Nonetheless, it would be prudent to check for yourself from time to time, just to make sure you're still getting the best deal.

Ask the right questions

When you're finally ready to pick up the phone and request flight information, you'll get a much better deal if you know the right questions to ask. Don't be afraid to nudge and prod your travel agent or airline representative to be sure you're getting information on all available bargain fares.

---

2 From "Airline Ticket Consolidators and Bucket Shops," FAQ, 2004, Edward Hasbrouck: *www.hasbrouck.org.*

The world of last-minute fares

By Lee Harrison

Not too long ago, I got an e-mail from US Airways advertising round-trip airfares to Gatwick airport near London or just $189. Since we were in the U.S. at the time, we left three days later for a wonderful five-day weekend in the Cotswolds. We also took advantage of another $240 US Airways fare to spend a long weekend in Madrid. From my home in Ecuador, we recently found a fare of $203 to New York on the airline Lan Chile. Such are the opportunities in the world of last-minute fares. They're not of much use for obligatory travel, but if you're flexible they represent a great opportunity for inexpensive and impulsive travel.

The way I find them is to sign up for the e-letters available from virtually every airline, foreign and domestic. Granted, I get more e-mail—I have a special e-mail address designated for this—but it's been worth it.

Another way to find last-minute fares is through services that search everyone's specials and send you a list periodically. Sherman's Travel does a good job at this, as does Bestfares.com. (See online resources in Appendix A.)

Here are a few things to ask:

- Would the fare be less expensive if I flew on a different day of the week? A different time of day? Or a different week of the month?

- Could I get a lower fare if I chose an earlier departure date?

- Are any special seasonal fares available?

- Are any promotional deals currently on offer?

- What is the off-peak fare?

- Is there any way that you know of that I could get a cheaper fare?

If you are dealing with a travel agent, be sure to ask about other airlines. Often, travel agents consistently promote certain airlines over others. But a travel agent should be able to quote you the fare to your destination on any airline that flies there.

Think ahead when it comes to flying with pets

If you are planning to bring your cat or dog on a flight with you, you must mention the fact when you are making your reservation. Most airlines charge about $80 each way for a cat or dog.

Only one dog is allowed to travel in the cabin on any given flight, (this is to prevent dogs from getting barking competitions going with each other), and no pets are allowed to travel in the cabin on transatlantic flights.

If your dog is small enough (i.e. very small), he can travel in a carrier that will fit under the seat in front of you. The same applies to cats, with just one cat per carrier, except in the case of kittens. Most airlines will allow two animals at most in coach, and one in business class. Animal travel is handled on a first-come, first-served basis, so get to the check-in desk early if you want your pet in the cabin with you.

If your dog is too big to fit in a carrier under a seat, he'll have to go in the pet area of the baggage section. This area is pressurized, but usually not temperature-controlled. It would be a lot better for your best friend if you were able to get a non-stop flight, as this area of the plane can get pretty hot when the plane is grounded in sunny places, and cold when it's flying over low-temperature climates.

Many airlines require that you have your pet sedated before you travel. Be warned: a lot of vets will grumble about this, as the animal is likely to become quite dehydrated, disoriented, and generally miserable. However, the upside is that once sedated, your pet won't be affected by travel sickness during the flight.

Flying with working dogs

Working dogs—i.e. guide dogs for the blind, signal dogs for the hard-of-hearing, and assistance dogs for mobility-impaired persons—travel with all U.S. airlines free of charge, and are allowed to accompany their owners into the cabin.

Shipping bicycles

Usually airlines will charge around $80 to ship a bicycle one way, but there are ways that you can save on this cost.

You can become a member of the **League of American Bicyclists**, *1612 K Street NW, Suite 800, Washington DC, 20006-2850; tel. 800-288-2453; fax 202-822-1334; website: www.bikeleague.org, email: bikeleague@bikeleague.org,* for a $25 annual fee ($30 for a family). Members receive free bike passes for U.S. Air, TWA, Northwest, and America West when they book their plane tickets through LAB's travel agency, the Sports National Reservation Center. Contact LAB for further information.

Bicycle transport for LAB members is free on most domestic flights operated by Frontier. You must make your reservation through **Adventure Travel**, *10909 Portland Avenue #R, Tacoma, Washington 98445; tel. 800-274-4567, or 253-531-1757; fax 253-531-9671.* Your bicycle can be substituted for one piece of check-in baggage (valid in 48 mainland states), and no minimum airfare is required. Be sure to package your bicycle properly for transport.

Brands of bikes such as Copilot and Bike Friday that can be disassembled and stored in their own cases, don't require you to pay the $50 each-way handling fee at Southwest Airlines.

LAB membership will also get you 5% to 10% off at a number of car rental companies, including Alamo, Hertz, Budget, and Dollar. Budget will also waive its additional fee for drivers under 25 years old.

A number of hotels around the world also offer discounts to LAB members. To avail of discounts on car rentals and hotels, you must book through **Navigant International**, *84 Inverness Circle East, Englewood, CO 80112, tel. (toll free) 800-225-0655, (toll free) 877-628-4426, or 303-706-0800; fax 303-706-0770; website: www.navigant.com.*

Organize your luggage and belongings

At present, the U.S. domestic baggage liability limit is a maximum of $1,250 per passenger, and some airlines may provide greater limits for checked/unchecked baggage. For international flights, the baggage liability limit is approximately $9.07 per pound ($20 per kilogram) for checked baggage, and $400 per passenger for unchecked baggage.

When you are declaring that a bag is lost, you will have to submit paperwork to the airline, listing the value of the bags and their contents. You won't necessarily receive the full value for all the lost items, and there is a minimum waiting period of one week before baggage can officially be declared lost. The good news is that about 98% of missing bags are reunited with their grateful owners. When this doesn't happen, reimbursement will come within two to six weeks.

Label your bags—if the airline can't identify the owner of a bag, it will be sent to a warehouse for three months, after which time anything in good condition will be sold at auction!

Be sure to remember: airlines will not reimburse you for currency, photographic, or electronic equipment (e.g., cameras, stereos, VCRs, camcorders, CD players, telephones, etc.), rare and expensive jewelry, artistic works, or medication, unless prior arrangements were made (e.g., excess valuation insurance was arranged). However, some credit card companies will cover these items if the flight tickets were purchased with their cards, so check with your credit card company to see what you would be entitled to claim, in the event of loss or breakage.

Report any damage to your bags, within seven days of receiving them; the airline will pay the cost of having them fixed or replaced, or give you new ones. If your bags are damaged before you check them, the airline is entitled to ask you to sign a damage waiver stating the nature of the damage, which will prevent you from claiming. You can't claim for normal wear and tear, and carry-on bags are not subject to damage claims, unless directly caused by a flight attendant.

Special meal requirements—take nothing for granted

Most major airlines will provide alternate meals on meal-flights, upon request, providing that the request is made **24 hours in advance**. Special meals include: Kosher, Muslim, Hindu, vegetarian, vegan, non-dairy, children's, low-fat, low-salt, low-cholesterol, low-calorie, low-carbohydrate, diabetic, fruit, low-gluten, sulfite-free, seafood, non-allergenic (e.g. nuts, shellfish) soft, and bland. Simply ask for the meal when you make your reservation; there is no extra charge.

If the airline forgets to load your special meal, ask for a meal voucher to be used at your destination airport. Even if you can't eat in the airport restaurants, you can buy nuts, candy, or fruit at the gift shops, and the airline will reimburse you the cost (within reason). Upon boarding the aircraft, you might even want to inform the flight attendant that you have special food-requirements, so that he/she can check to see if your meal has been loaded, while there is still a chance to get it brought on-board.

Coordinating and scheduling menus for airlines is an epic task, so even on good days you have a fair chance of not getting the meal you requested. If you have dietary restrictions, it's best to bring your own food in case the airline doesn't load your meal—particularly on longer flights, where you might go hungry otherwise.

Chapter 2

Web-based travel services

Web-based travel services are becoming more and more popular, efficient, and competitive these days, and they're a good place to do comparative price shopping. Each service has its particular strengths and weaknesses, and the truth is, where you end up buying your ticket is much less important than the process you use to get there. Let's take a look at a few tricks to find the best airfares.

Don't worry if you've never used a web-based travel service, or if you don't consider yourself particularly Internet-savvy: we'll give you a brief lesson later on in this chapter.

How to get started

First, choose a web-based travel service with a "your dates are flexible" option. You'll see this option where you have to specify the date you're going. If you indicate that your dates are flexible, the system will then list all the fares available between your departure and arrival airports. Then, you pick from the dates with the lowest fares.

Due to date restrictions on some fares, you may not always be able to use the cheapest one, but rest assured, you'll almost never find the lowest fare by plugging in exact dates and seeing which fares come up. Even when we've known that a certain low fare existed, we've sometimes found it very difficult to reproduce it on the airline's own website after finding it on a web-based travel service. Travelocity's website is a good place to experiment. You can see the lowest fares between two cities, and when they're available.

Once you've got these low-fare dates, you can then enter them into websites that don't have the "flexible dates" option to see if they offer even cheaper prices.

If you have to travel on a specific day and at a certain time, you'll probably find similar results on any of the major travel sites (though they all have exclusive deals from time to time). Ask yourself whether you have a little flexibility, though, even a day or two. Sometimes when using "flexible dates," you can travel on or very close to the days you had in mind anyway, and come up with a much cheaper fare.

Here's where some of the major travel websites stand with respect to flexible date planning:

- **Travelocity:** Supports flexible dates for all flights, worldwide.

- **Bestfares:** Supports flexible dates for many using the Quickfare Finder, which searches for flights in the Western Hemisphere, and soon in Europe too.

- **Orbitz:** Flexible dates available for flights in the U.S. and Canada.

- **Expedia:** Flexible dates available only on their "most popular routes."

- **Priceline:** Dates must be specified and departure city must be within the U.S.

- **SideStep:** Dates must be specified.

Additionally, many airline websites offer flexible date planning, but you must of course look at each airline individually. A word of caution here on the posted prices: when using the flexible date option, many of the taxes and fees are not added onto the fare until you select your flights. So it may appear that Travelocity (as an example) is cheaper when you get the search results, but once you've selected your flights they'll be right up there with everyone else.

Making your final choice

Once you've been presented with an itinerary, take a close look at the cities again. Some services will route you to a nearby alternative airport automatically. While all will notify you that they've done it, it's sometimes easy to miss.

At times, your departure airport and your return airport may be different. For example, American Airlines will sometimes schedule your departure from New York's JFK, and your return trip's arrival to LaGuardia. When this happens, you need to double-check your rental car options to make sure that they consider this the "same location." If not, you could lose your airfare savings to a higher rental car cost.

Before actually buying a ticket from anyone, it's a good idea to cross-check what you've come up with against another service or two. If you've found a good fare using Travelocity for example, you can take your results and go to Expedia, Orbitz, or one of many other excellent travel sites.

No matter which site you're working with, it's a good idea to allow SideStep to analyze where you're going, to try to get a better price. The prices are often the same, but they'll occasionally save you significant money both on airfares and hotels. Also, SideStep is a great option when you've got to travel on specific dates and times, since it analyzes so many independent sites. See the close of this chapter for more info on SideStep.

Once you've made your choice, you can buy e-tickets online, and print the confirmation, which is required to enter some airports. We recommend e-tickets because they're easy to change if necessary, impossible to lose, and now even cost less than a paper ticket.

Using a web-based travel service

The nice thing about making travel arrangements online is that most of the travel services work the same way. You enter your departure and arrival cities (and sometimes the dates of travel) and you'll be presented with a list of options. Typically, they'll give you departure and arrival times, layover times, flight numbers, etc. Car rental services tell you the size, models, and prices, while hotel booking services give you room and property information.

These services also provide any special rules or restrictions that apply to the fare you select, such as weekend stays, number of stopovers, and validity dates for open-ended travel. Simply select the least expensive option that meets your needs.

Once you've selected your flight—and car or hotel—you'll be given a chance to enter your payment information. Usually, you can store your credit card info with the company to make this easier. We've found this practice to be safe, and since 1991, we have never had a problem with online booking security.

How to request your flight

Let's try a sample trip using Travelocity's system as an example— but remember that they all work pretty much the same way.

- Go to *www.travelocity.com* and on the first screen simply enter your "To" and "From" cities, as either airport codes or complete names. We'd recommend that when starting your search, you always check the box that says your dates are flexible, even if they're not. At times, you'll find that a lower fare comes up that is available on your travel dates that does not come up when you specify those same dates. (Travelocity now offers an option for people traveling within the U.S. and Canada to "Compare Surrounding airport" prices. This is presented as an alternative to the "Flexible dates" option.) Once you've entered your cities, click "search flights."

- The next screen you'll see will be a listing of the available flights, sorted by fare, with the lowest fares being presented first. Take a look at the right side of the page, and you'll see some brief information telling you about dates of travel, length of stay, etc. You can click on "Rules" for more detailed info. Click on a flight to continue your search.

- Now you'll see three months of calendars, showing you the dates on which your fare is available. Just click on your desired departure date, and when the next screen appears, click on your desired return date. If one of the dates you select is sold out, you'll be shown the nearest available dates. If what's available doesn't meet your needs, just hit the "Back" button on your browser until you see the list of flights, and then pick another one. Don't forget, though, that when using the "flexible dates" option, it's only after you've chosen your specific flight that the posted price will include taxes and fees. (The original fare you saw was the base price.) Use this complete price for comparison purposes. If you specified exact dates from the beginning, you'll have seen the all-inclusive price right away, and may have missed a lower fare.

- Once you've picked your dates of travel, you'll be presented with the different flights that are available on those dates. Pick the one you want—if there's more than one—and you'll be walked through the (optional) seat selection and (required) payment process.

Keep an eye on frequent destinations with "alerts"

Many of the online travel services and airline sites also have an "alert" system for fare watching. Using these alerts, you can specify several of your frequent destinations, and the site will continually display the best available price. Some sites, such as Travelocity, will even send you an e-mail if one of your cities drops in price by an amount you specify. This is particularly handy for visits to parents, children, and other trips that don't have a mandatory travel date.

See **Appendix A** for a list of some of the most popular online travel sites.

But what about low-cost airlines not featured on websites?

You'll hear a lot of talk about the great deals available from airlines that don't show up on the online travel sites...airlines such as Southwest or JetBlue. While it's true that their prices are consistently low, you can sometimes beat them with some advance planning. Let us give you the results of a little test:

When comparing a flight from New York to the Dominican Republic: American Airlines was charging $331, while Travelocity found the exact same flight for $327. On a flight from Boston to Oakland: JetBlue was $332, while Travelocity (via American West) was just $282. A sample itinerary from Phoenix to Detroit found that Southwest priced the trip at $343...but Travelocity (via American Airlines) was just $214.

Granted, these are all great prices, and for the most part, pretty close. The lesson here is that you should never assume that you've found the one, cheapest travel service. Even though Southwest or JetBlue often have the best fares to the cities they serve, they're not unbeatable.

SideStep search engine

This is a service, in which a small program is downloaded to your PC. Once installed, SideStep will pop up whenever it sees that you're entering dates and cities on an airline or travel website, and ask if you'd like it to compare prices. When you click "yes," it will go out and search hundreds of other websites looking for the best fare.

It works not only for airlines, but for cars and hotels as well.

In addition to the pop-up feature, you can also go directly to SideStep and perform your searches at *www.sidestep.com*, but you'll still need the program if you want to compare prices side-by-side with other travel sites.

When you select an option from SideStep, they don't actually sell you a ticket, but rather forward you automatically to the provider's website for purchase, whether it be an airline, hotel, or car rental. All fees and taxes are included in their price quotes. For hotel searches, Travelaxe works the same way, which you can find at *www.travelaxe.com*.

Chapter 3

Alternative agents

Y ou can save a great deal of money on every airfare you buy—as much as 50% and more—by dealing with alternative agencies, such as bucket shops and consolidators. It is no more difficult or inconvenient to deal with a discount agency than with your neighborhood travel agent. It can, however, be slightly more risky.

Most discount agencies are entirely legitimate. However, they are independent outfits, and it is not unusual for them to suddenly go out of business. As we've already explained, always use a credit card when dealing with these alternative agencies. And always ask for—and take the time to check—references from a local airline.

If you're having trouble with some of the terms, like bucket shop and consolidator, you're not alone. According to author, essayist, and professional travel agent Edward Hasbrouck [3], there is no industry standard definition for these operations, and their usage varies. Mr. Hasbrouck's concise definitions are probably the best available:

"Generally speaking, consolidators are agencies that have discount agreements with the airlines. In most cases, especially within the U.S., consolidators are wholesalers who sell only through retail travel agencies, not directly to the public."

"Bucket shops are retail agencies that specialize in knowing the full range of consolidators (every airline has many consolidators) and in

---

[3] Edward Hasbrouck is the author of *The Practical Nomad* series of travel guides.

knowing other techniques of fare construction, routing, etc. for discount prices."

For more information on bucket shops and consolidators—as well as a wealth of other travel info—take a look at *www.hasbrouck.org*.

Consolidators

Consolidators handle a high volume of passengers and usually specialize in travel to specific countries or regions. They receive commissions from the airlines they work with and rebate much of that money to their clients. Some consolidators work only with travel agents; others also sell to the public. In addition to offering 20% to 40% discounts off published fares, consolidators are also able to waive advance-purchase requirements and minimum- and maximum-stay limits. That New York-to-London, round-trip, economy-class airfare your regular travel agent told you would cost $600? A consolidator might sell the same ticket for about $400.

Here are some popular consolidators:

- **Air Brokers International,** *tel. (800)833-3273.*

- **AirlineConsolidator.com,** *tel. (888)468-5385.*

- **TFI Tours International Ltd.,** *tel. (800)745-8000*

Bucket shops

Enormous discounts (up to two-thirds off) are not unusual on tickets from overseas discount travel agencies, known as bucket shops. Low overhead, and high-volume sales keep prices low. Although they sell scheduled flights with major airlines, the cheapest flights are sometimes with lesser-known (often from developing nations or East European countries) airlines. Bucket shops are particularly useful for planning difficult itineraries and "round-the-world" (RTW) trips.

Before you take advantage of the bargains, be aware of the drawbacks peculiar to this kind of operation. Bucket shops are not always licensed and bonded, and cancelation penalties are high. And remember, small airlines from developing countries do not follow the same safety standards adhered to by the major international airlines.

London bucket shops are advertised in:

- **Time Out Magazine,** *Universal House, 251 Tottenham Court Road, London W1T 7AB; tel. (44)207-813-3000; website: www.timeout.com.*

- **The Evening Standard Associated Newspapers,** *Northclisse House, 2 Derry St., Kensington W85EE; tel. (44)207-938-6000; website: www.esadvertising.co.uk.*

The following bucket shops take major credit cards and will send tickets to you in the U.S.:

- **Air Travel Advisory Bureau;** *tel. (44)207-636-5000; website: www.atab.com.*

- **Destination Group**, *41/45 Goswell Road, London AC1, England; tel. (44)207-636-5000.*

- **Worldwide Cheap Travel**, *254 Earls Court Road, London SW5 9AD; tel. (44)207-373-6465.*

- **Latitude 40**, *13 Beauchamp Place, Knightsbridge, London SW3 1NQ; tel. (44)207-581-1879.* (Mainly for travel to Spain and Portugal.)

The following U.S. shops are worth a look as well:

- **Air Brokers International**, *685 Market St., Suite 400, San Francisco, CA 94105, U.S.; tel. (800)883-3273 or (415)397-1383; fax: (415)397-4767; website: www.airbrokers.com.* Office hours are Monday through Friday 8:30 a.m. to 5:30 p.m. Accepts checks, Visa, Mastercard, and AmEx with a 3% surcharge.

- **Airtreks High Adventure Travel** (Jesse Walkershaw and Edward Hasbrouck), *301 Howard Street, 4th Floor, San Francisco, CA, 94102; tel. (800)350-0612, (800)AIRTREKS or (415)977-7100; e-mail: airtreks@highadv.com; website: www.airtreks.com.* Office hours are Monday through Friday, 9 a.m. to 6 p.m. Visits by appointment only. Accepts checks, Visa, Mastercard, and AmEx with 3% surcharge.

- **Avia Travel**, *1029 Solaro Ave., Suite E-Albany, CA 94706, U.S.; tel. (800)950-2842 or (510)558-2150; fax; (510)558-2158; website: www.aviatravel.com.* Specializes in Asia, but also does RTWs.

- **DIA International Travel,** *P.O. Box 39105, Washington, D.C. 20016; tel. (800)342-8258 or (202)342-8687; fax: (202)625-0288; website: www.diatravel.com.*

- **JustFares.com,** *3123 Eastlake Ave E Seattle,WA 98102; tel. (800)766-3601, or (206) 223-3600; website: www.justfares.com.* No credit card fees, no last-minute fees, no delivery fees.

Flying on charters

Charter flights are often good deals. Charter operators arrange flights and hotels between heavily traveled routes. By moving large numbers of travelers every week over these routes, they can get huge price reductions—and pass them on to customers.

But there are drawbacks. You must get to the departure city for the charter tour on your own. If you cancel after you have paid for a charter trip, you usually lose the entire amount. Refunds are very uncommon. Most companies advertise base prices, add fees (usually 15% of the base figures), and then tack on surcharges, making it difficult to find the actual total cost until it's too late to back out. If you are traveling alone, you should be aware that most charter companies also add single supplements which can run to a few hundred dollars.

You also should realize that operators can cancel charters up to 10 days before the date of departure, and the flight times and dates can be changed any time. Furthermore, charter operators can increase the price of trips by as much as 10%, up to 10 days before departure. Finally, if you miss your plane, you can't catch the next one out. There is no next plane out—these are not regularly scheduled flights.

Don't be completely turned off by charters, despite our warnings. Many people use charters routinely, and save a lot of money doing so, using the same ones over and over again to their frequent destinations.

Don't book a charter—no matter how attractive the savings seem—

without doing a quick background check. Surf on the Internet to see if anyone has complained about the carrier and why. Also, ask the charter company whether it is a member of a professional association, then ask the association whether the company is indeed a member in good standing.

Here are a few air charters to consider:

- **Apple Vacations,** *toll-free tel. (866)265-2651 or (281)265-2651; website: www.affordable-vacations.com.* Offers scheduled and charter flights to Mexico, Hawaii, Bahamas, Bermuda, Costa Rica, the Caribbean, and more.

- **Air Charter United,** *tel. (877)BIDJETS or (305)885-6665; fax: (305)885-6664; email: info@aircharterunited.com, website: www. aircharterunited.com.*

Never pay in cash

Pay with plastic. It is to your advantage to pay for your air travel with a credit card for many reasons:

✓It's easy. You can make all the arrangements over the telephone or Internet.

✓Refunds are speedier. Airlines must refund tickets purchased by credit card within seven days. This is not the case if a ticket is paid for by cash or check. (For this reason, if you are dealing with travel agents, make sure they pay for your ticket with your credit card number.)

✓You can get credit for the ticket if the airline goes bankrupt.

✓The ticket number of your flight will be printed on your credit card bill. If you lose a paper ticket, this makes it much easier to have it replaced. It can also make it easier to find your records online, if you need to claim frequent flyer miles or ask for a refund.

✓If your ticket is stolen, the thief cannot cash it in for a monetary refund; the refund can only be credited to your credit card account.

✓You get automatic insurance coverage. Check with your credit card company for specifics on the coverage available to you.

✓More frequent flyer miles. Many programs allow you to accrue miles every time you use their credit card to pay for travel. (See Chapter Seven for details.)

✓You minimize the risk in dealing with bucket shops, and charter airlines (which are discussed in this book). Play it safe by paying with a credit card.

Chapter 4

Alternative ticketing

You can save money, travel farther, stay longer, and avoid many airline restrictions if you understand the ins and outs of the ticketing process. Most travelers are unaware of certain angles, or tricks, of the airline trade—such as split ticketing, hub ticketing, and maximum permitted mileage—that savvy shoppers consistently use to tremendous advantage.

Split ticketing

Split ticketing, or currency differential ticketing, can save you a substantial amount of money on international flights, especially if you're flying first class, business class, or full-fare coach. You purchase two separate one-way tickets instead of a round-trip (the outbound ticket in the U.S. where you pay in dollars), and you buy a one-way flight back in local currency. Check the fare of your return flight first to see whether the savings will be significant, which they usually are.

For example, a round-trip ticket from New York to Paris flying business class would cost you almost $6,000. But if you buy the one-way flight for $3,000 and the return for £1,190 (equal to $2,100), you'll be saving $900.

A slight variation on this theme is to use discounted, promotional round-trip fares as one-way tickets. If you need a one-way ticket, you'll sometimes find that the discounted round-trip ticket is less than a one-way ticket. In this case, you just discard the return ticket. (You can no longer discard the outbound and use the return as was possible in the past, since your reservation will be canceled when you don't use the outbound.)

Maximum permitted mileage and stopovers

A technique known as maximum permitted mileage allows you to lengthen an international flight by adding stopovers, arranging variations in your travel route, even switching airlines.

Why would you want to add miles to a trip? Consider this: You're flying from New York to Scandinavia. By arranging to reroute the trip through London, and arranging for a stopover there, you get to visit London for free.

There is a limit to the number of miles you can add onto a ticket, and airline restrictions affect rerouting and stopovers, so this isn't an easy thing to arrange. You need the help of a creative travel agent who is familiar with airline routes.

On the other hand, the online travel services will tell you how many stopovers are permitted, and how long they can be. If there's a charge for stopovers, you'll see that, too. Just click on the "Rules" link that normally appears with the flight selections. All you usually need to do is make the reservation online, then call the airlines and inform them of which stopovers you'll be taking advantage of. (We've not found any way to actually schedule the stopovers online.) The airline agent will make the necessary changes.

Taking advantage of the maximum permitted mileage makes even more sense if you belong to a frequent flyer program. The more miles you fly the more frequent flyer points you'll rack up.

Hub ticketing

All airlines have host, or hub cities, out of which they base their routes. From this hub city, the airline flies directly to all the other cities it services. Therefore, many airlines find it more functional—and less expensive—to fly passengers back to the hub city instead of directly to cities that aren't on their standard routes. Passengers then continue their flights from the airline's home base. When booking a flight, ask for the fare for a flight via the airline's hub city. Compare this with the cost of flying directly to your destination. The savings sometimes can make up for the additional flight and the stopover.

If you're booking online, try booking one flight to and from the hub city, and another round-trip flight from the hub city to your destination. Since discounts are more common when the hub city is involved, this can be quite a bit cheaper.

The virtues of getting bumped

Airlines typically overbook their flights by up to 20%, knowing that a certain number of paying passengers will not show up. Sometimes though, more passengers than usual show up and airline officials are faced with 200 seats and 205 passengers, five of whom are likely to become very annoyed. That's where you come in.

The basic rule is that if an airline bumps you, it is required to cover the cost of your flight, as long as you are holding a paid ticket and had a confirmed reservation, and as long as you met the gate check-in deadline for the flight. (Be careful: this doesn't just mean the time you check in at the ticket counter or check your baggage. It's the time you arrive at the departure gate.) If the airline can get you out on another flight—either its flight or that of another airline—within one hour of your original flight time, it owes you nothing. But this virtually never happens. If it can get you out up to two hours after your original flight time, they must reimburse you for the cost of your one-way fare up to $200. If it takes more than two hours, you are entitled to twice the value of your one-way fare up to $400. They might even offer you a free flight.

This is how it works if you are bumped involuntarily.

Voluntary bumping, on the other hand, is where you are asked to give up your seat on an overbooked flight. There is no minimum or maximum cap on what the airline has to offer you in return for your

How I got bumped...
and what to do if it happens to you
By Len Galvin

I was in Copenhagen airport, waiting for a flight to Moscow with SAS (the Swedish air carrier). A flight attendant started working her way through the seating area (my friend and I were about third in line) talking to people, asking them if they wanted to take a later flight. It seems SAS had oversold the flight—air carriers do this all the time.

When she offered each of us a $200 voucher if we'd change our flight, we hesitated. Organizing our trip to Russia had involved a lot of red tape, and we weren't sure if it would make a difference to the Russians that we might arrive on a different flight than the one we had said in the various forms we filled out. But then she upped it to a $400 voucher each, so we took our chances.

A few things to bear in mind if this ever happens to you...and if you do any amount of regular travel, it will:

✓Read the fine print. Different airlines will have different bumping policies. SAS, for example, will offer you flight vouchers, which you can use to pay for SAS flights or exchange for half their value in cash. (We used them to take a fishing trip to the Arctic Circle.) Find out the policy on the vouchers before you agree to anything: when the vouchers expire, what their cash equivalent is, and if there are any exclusions.

✓Remember who's doing whom a favor. The airline is asking you to help them fix a mistake they made. Hold out for the best deal possible. We only hesitated a few seconds and doubled our compensation, and I'm sure we could have done even better if we had the presence of mind to play hardball. Other methods of compensation can include free upgrades, cash/voucher combinations, and VIP lounge access.

✓Be flexible. If you agree to be bumped from your flight, part of the deal is that the airline will do their best to get you to where you're going—as close as possible to the time you're meant to arrive—but your original plans will still change. This means you could now have extra transfers, later departure and arrival times, and no special meals. If you (or your group) can't be flexible and take things as they come, then maybe you should rethink giving up your seat.

seat, so you can play this situation to your advantage. The airline might offer a free round-trip flight. If this happens, make sure they guarantee you a confirmed seat, not standby. Some people even make a habit of getting voluntarily bumped on a regular basis, and before they know it they've collected enough vouchers for a family holiday.

If the free ticket is in the form of a voucher, make sure it's an unrestricted voucher—some vouchers only allow standby travel or have blackout dates when they cannot be used. If the wait between flights is going to be long, request some other form of entitlement such as free meals or phone calls.

In the event that no one offers to be bumped voluntarily, the airline will sweeten the rewards. An airline will sometimes offer a voucher of

One-pence flights, courtesy of Ryanair
By Laura Sheridan

I'm off to Italy next week. My four flights (two each way) cost me four pence sterling...that's about six cents. And, no, it's not a typo. I'll fly from Dublin to London, and then London to Trieste, in northern Italy. (Trieste is on the border with Slovenia, so I'll get to see this beautiful country as well.) Coming back, I'll fly from Venice to London, and then back to Dublin. Four flights altogether, at one pence per flight.

Truth be told, this excludes the tax. The total cost to me will in fact be £90, but still, what a bargain. All this courtesy of Ryanair, the Irish airline that is making a name (and a market) for itself with these kind of you-can't-believe-it deals. Ryanair covers most of Europe, including Italy, Belgium, France, Spain, and Germany.

To get a deal like I just got, you have to book online at the Ryanair web-site, *www.ryanair.com*, you have to be flexible, and you have to book well in advance. I think I got in just in time the day I booked my flights. I've just been to Ryanair's website again, and the one-pence flights are gone. There are still really cheap flights, though, including one from London to Paris for £5 (about $9.10). And if you check on a regular basis, you're sure to see these one-pence flights again.

between $500 and $1,000, as well as the free flight, depending on how desperate it gets.

Whether you are bumped voluntarily or involuntarily, make sure the gate agent protects all your connecting or subsequent flights. Otherwise, you could be listed on the airline's computer as a no-show, and have your subsequent itinerary canceled.

Chapter 5

Bargain fares for special groups

I f you are a senior citizen, a student, disabled, or a member of a travel club, you can avail of benefits such as discount rates and special offers when you travel. The only problem with these special offers is that people often don't know they exist, and so are unaware of what they're missing. Read on for a good outline of some of the best specialty travel programs available today.

Senior citizens

What follows is a list of airlines that offer discounts to senior citizens:

- **American Airlines** offers senior fares in most domestic markets for seniors 65 and older. *Tel. (800)433-7300; website: www.aa.com.*

- **Continental** offers senior fares to selected destinations for passengers 65 and older. Ask for details when you make your reservation. When booking online select the "Seniors" category. *Tel. (800)525-0280; website: www.continental.com.*

- **United** offers the Silver Wings program to travelers 55 and older. United also offers discounts on car rentals and hotels. *Tel. (214)760-0022; website: www.ual.com.*

- **SAS (Scandinavian Airlines)**, for those aged 65 or over, a 35% discount is available on most SAS Economy Class fares from the UK and Ireland to Scandinavia and Finland. Gives senior citizens additional travel discounts as members of senior travel clubs, which offer discount rates on transportation, including airfare. *Tel. (800)221-2350.*

One of the best deals out there is **Elderhostel**, which arranges study tours for travelers over 55. You can learn the art of French cooking at an 18th-century château near Paris, or study antiques and collectibles at a stately home in London. Participants stay in dormitories during the courses. A catalog lists more than 20,000 educational opportunities in Europe, Australia, Scandinavia, and the U.S. For more information, contact **Elderhostel,** *11 Avenue de Lafayette Boston, MA 02111-1746; tel. (877)426-8056; fax: (877)426-2166.*

Youth programs

A child under the age of 12 may be eligible for discounted travel, depending on the airline. If the child is traveling with an adult paying full fare, discounts can be 25% to 50%. Young people aged 12 to 25 sometimes can apply for youth discounts as well, even if they are not active students. These offers change often, so ask specifically about youth discounts when booking your flight. If you are an active student, you have the world at your fingertips. Throughout Europe and much of Latin America, student IDs for students of any age qualify travelers for discounts on transportation, meals, and entry fees to museums and movies.

Following is a list of organizations that offer discounts to student travelers, including airfare discounts:

- **American Intercultural Student Exchange**, *707 Lakehall Rd., Lake Village, AR 71653; tel. (870)265-5050; fax: (870)265-5001; website:www.aise.com.*

- **American Youth Hostels**, *733 15th Street N.W., Suite 840,Washington, D.C. 20005; tel. (202)783-6161.* These are open to everyone regardless of age.

- **Canadian Hostelling Association**, *400-205 Catherine St., Ottawa, Ontario K2P1C3, Canada; tel. (613)237-7884.* All ages can participate.

- **Council on International Educational Exchange (CIEE)**,

205 E. 42nd St., 14th Floor, New York, NY 10017; tel. (212)822-2600. This youth travel agency helps students find temporary employment overseas.

- **International Christian Youth Exchange,** *134 W. 26th St., NewYork, NY 10001; tel. (212)206-7307.* This group arranges international exchange programs.

- **Youth for Understanding,** *6400 Goldsboro Rd., Ste 100. Bethesda, MD 20817; tel. (800)TEENAGE.* This organization works with the U.S. Department of State to arrange international exchange programs for teenagers from 15 to 18 years old.

In addition, travel offices that are associated with the International Student Travel Confederation (ISTC) give students special deals on flights. On offer are cheap and flexible flight tickets to hundreds of destinations. The International Student Identity Card (ISIC), through ISTC, is an internationally recognized student ID card that entitles the bearer to discounts on flights and other modes of transport in 106 countries worldwide. As well as offering substantial discounts, these tickets allow you to change your plans along the way, often without incurring any financial penalties. Most of the fares are negotiated through the Student Air Travel Association (SATA).

The benefits of these tickets are:

- Built-in flexibility allows you to change travel dates and routes either free-of-charge, or for a minimal fee.

- Unused portions of your ticket may be refunded.

- You can fly into one city and return from another.

- All the participating airlines are well established and reliable.

- Some tickets are valid for up to a year.

- Discounts are widely available on buses, trains, and ferries.

- Discounts are available on entrance to the world's leading museums and cultural sites, entertainment and attractions (including cinemas), as well as accommodation in youth hostels and some hotels.

- Discounts are given in some bars and restaurants, and more commonly in stores.

Full-time students of any age, and anyone (including non-students) aged 12 to 26 can apply for an ISIC card. The cost is $22, and membership must be renewed annually.

Discount cards for educators

If you are a full-time teacher or professor, the International Youth Travel Card (IYTC) or International Teacher Identity Card (ITIC) will be well worth having. These cards offer similar benefits, services and savings to the ISIC card. The cost is $22, payable annually for each card.

Check the websites: *www.isic.org* and *www.istc.org* for information about ISIC and ISTC offices in your area, and for application details for ISIC, IYTC, and ITIC cards.

Disabled travelers

For details on discounts, amenities, and sevices for disabled travelers, contact the following organizations:

- **Flying Wheels Travel**, *143 W. Bridge St., Box 382, Owatonna, MN 55060; tel. (507)451-5005; fax (507)451-1685; website: www.flyingwheelstravel.com; e-mail: thq@llnet.* A tour operator and travel agency that specializes in travel for people with disabilities—includes accessible cruises.

- **Mobility International U.S.A.**, *P.O. Box 10767, Eugene, or 97440; tel. (541)343-1284; website: www.miusa.org.* An information service for travelers with disabilities. It also operates educational exchange programs specializing in cultural diversity, home stays, and leadership.

- **Travel Information Service**, *Moss Rehabilitation Hospital, 1200 W Tabor Road Philadelphia, PA 19141, tel. (215)456-9600; website: www.mossresourcenet.org/travel.* This is not a travel agency, however it offers a wealth of travel information for the disabled.

Air travel clubs

Another good way to enjoy tremendous discounts on your air travel is by joining an air-travel club. Some of these clubs charge high enrollment fees as well as yearly dues. Nonetheless, they can save you money. Following are two clubs that do not charge exorbitant fees, and are consistently popular with members.

- **Shillelagh Travel Club,** *100 East Street, SE, Suite 302, Vienna, Virginia 22180-4800; tel. (703)242-2204 or (toll free) 800-556-846; fax: (703)242-2781; website: www.shillelaghtravelclub.com.* This club caters for families, couples, and singles (generally 50 years plus). The annual fee is $35 for singles, and $50 for families (two or more members). When a member reserves his/her first overnight trip, he/she will get free one-year membership. The club can match you with a roommate for your trips, or provide you with single accommodation. Past trips include Ireland, and the Bahamas.

- **Women's Travel Club,** *tel. (toll free) 800-480-4448; website: www.womenstravelclub.com; e-mail: womantrip@aol.com.* Membership costs $35 annually (or $65 for two years). This club has a lot of info for the female traveler, including bulletin boards and member-contributed articles. Each year the club organizes 25 to 30 trips: from straightforward spa trips at a discount, to four-night trips to Costa Rica, Mexico, and London. They also take longer trips to India, and China, as well as multi-city trips. Members receive coupons and special offers.

Chapter 6

Travel with a pass

One of the most inexpensive and convenient ways we know of to travel independently in a specific country or region is with a travel pass. Air travel passes allow multiple stops, unlimited flights, and discounts on flights within various countries. They are most useful in large countries, in countries where cities are widely separated with little to see in between, and in groups of countries, such as Scandinavia. They can also be helpful when you want to see a country thoroughly in a short time.

The primary advantage however, is the cost. Airfare passes can cost half to one-third as much as you'd pay if you purchased each fare individually. Most air travel passes carry restrictions. Many must be purchased outside the country they are valid for, and some require that you arrive on the national carrier of the destination country. Following is a run-down of the major air passes on offer right now:

- **AUSTRALIA. Qantas Air** offers the Boomerang pass for travel within Australia, New Zealand, or South West Pacific; approx. $190 for a one-zone travel pass, and $240 for two-zone travel pass (there are five zones in all). *Tel. (toll free) 800-227-4500; website: www.qantas.com.*

- **BRAZIL. Varig** offers a pass to any five cities good for 21 days for $440. You cannot backtrack. The pass must be issued in the U.S., and is valid for one year if unopened. *Tel. (800)GO-VARIG; website: www.varig.com.*

- **CHILE. LAN Chile** offers several varieties of passes. *Tel. (800)735-5526; website: www.lanchile.com.*

- **EUROPE. Europebyair.com** lets you hop around Europe for just $99 per flight. Open passes allow you to fly one-way to cities all over Europe, starting and ending anywhere you want. *Website: www.europebyair.com.*

- **INDIA. Air India's** Discover India pass costs $750 and comes with unlimited travel for 21 days; no backtracking. A 15-day pass is $500. *Tel. (212)751-6200; website: www.airindia.com.*

- **NEW ZEALAND. Air New Zealand** offers a South Pacific Airpass for travel to 36 destinations in New Zealand, Australia, and the Pacific Islands for holders of an international plane ticket to New Zealand. Various one-way tickets are offered, ranging from $79 to $549. Through Star Alliance, the airline offers a similar Star Alliance South Pacific Airpass. *Tel. (800)262-1234; website: www.airnz.com.*

- **SCANDINAVIA. SAS** offers several different kinds of air passes, to Scandinavia, the Baltics, and Europe. *Tel. (800)221-2350; website: www.scandinavian.net.*

- **SOUTH PACIFIC. Air Promotions (APS), Inc. North America** is a general sales agent for a number of South Pacific Airlines: Air Nauru, Air Vanuatu, Polynesian Airlines and Soloman Airlines. *Website: www.pacificislands.com/air_passes/air_passes.html.*

Around-the-world fares

It may seem like taking the long way 'round, but an around-the-world airfare sometimes can be cheaper than a round-trip fare if you're flying from one side of the world to the other, or if you're planning an extended trip to several different cities. When flying on an around-the-world airfare, you must adhere to the following restrictions:

- You can stop in each city only once.

- In most cases, you must travel continuously eastward or continuously westward.

- You must complete your travel within a specified time frame, usually six months to a year.

There are numerous advantages in addition to the cost savings. You are allowed unlimited stopovers and you may even be able to backtrack, or add flights, and still save money. And because the first leg of an around-the-world trip is the only one that requires advance confirmation, your schedule is flexible. International carriers cooperate to offer around-the-world flights, since no airline flies to all corners of the globe.

Following are two associated airlines offering around-the-world itineraries, and the associate airlines they work with:

- **Star Alliance:** Air Canada, Lufthansa, Air New Zealand, Asiana Airlines, Singapore Airlines, LOT Polish Airlines, US Airways, and more; *website: www.star-alliance.com.*

- **Skyteam:** AeroMexico, Air France, Alitalia, Czech Airlines, and Korean Air; *website: www.skyteam.com.*

Some discount ticket agencies also specialize in around-the-world flights. **Contact Air Brokers International,** *tel. (800)883-3273; website: www.airbrokers.com.*

Chapter 7

The advantages of frequent flyer programs

I f anyone should go down in history as the marketing genius of all time, it could be the person who came up with the idea for the first frequent flyer (FF) program

American Airlines started its first frequent flyer program in 1981, to build customer loyalty, and the other major airlines weren't long catching on. Today there are over 70 frequent flyer programs, and they give away more than 10 million free tickets every year. Every day, employees spend a lot of time and effort trying to steer the company travel consultants toward the airlines where they have their "miles."

Airline FF programs, which award points toward free flights each time you fly, are most advantageous for business travelers and those people who do a significant amount of traveling. That said, they can benefit almost anyone, and no one should take a flight without having signed up for the airline's FF program. If you decline to join on the first flight because you "don't normally take this airline," fate will have you on that airline again before too long. In addition to flying, it's also possible to accumulate frequent flyer miles by using some credit cards, staying at certain hotels, renting cars from particular agencies, and even shopping in certain stores.

Frequent flyer programs also offer different membership levels to reward the most frequent customers. These offer additional benefits, like preferred customer phone numbers, preferred boarding, accelerated upgrade and mileage accrual, and preference when requesting upgrades.

Most major airlines also have a newsletter associated with their FF program, which is a great way to stay in touch with what the program offers, rule changes, as well as last minute specials, and other travel bargains. The more FF memberships you have, the better your chances are of catching a good deal that really strikes your fancy.

Typically the programs give you something to the effect of a free U.S. domestic roundtrip for 20,000 miles flown, a ticket to Hawaii or the Caribbean for 30,000, a ticket to Europe for 40,000, and a ticket to Australia or Asia for 60,000. Mileage levels vary across airlines.

A few things to watch out for

If you happen to catch an earlier flight than the one you had original-

Departures for the dearly departed— dead beneficial to undertakers

Whether anyone likes it or not, transporting human remains is a growth area for airlines, and quite a lucrative business niche, as families are more and more spread out, and retirees are increasingly moving abroad, but opting to be buried back home. Delta, for example, carried about 50,000 corpses a year: that volume accounted for about 10% of the airline's total cargo.

It's estimated that an airline would have to ship about 1,000 pounds of ordinary cargo to generate the same revenue as one dead body. A Florida to New York shipment would generally cost the buyer $250 to $380, and the price is ultimately determined by weight, distance, and demand. (Florida provides an important market; 14% of people who died there in 2003 were shipped to another state to be buried.)

Undertakers benefit from what some people grimly refer to as frequent "dier" programs. They can collect miles every time they transport a corpse, and the undertaker who receives the body, as well as the one who receives it, gets points from the airline that was used. JetBlue, for example, currently give a free round-trip ticket to a mortuary once it has undertaken 15 ship-outs with them.

So, although the families of the deceased pay for the flights, the undertakers rack up the mileage, and benefit from getting lots of free flights every year, enough in fact to treat their secretaries, and their families from time to time.

ly booked, be sure that your frequent flyer number is recorded again. The numbers may not necessarily transfer from one record to another when you change flights. If you notice that this happened, send a copy of your ticket receipt and boarding pass to the airline to get your mileage recorded.

It's worth just checking that your frequent flyer number is recorded every time you are dealing with a ticket-handler—i.e. when you make reservations, when you check in, and when you arrive at the gate for each flight you must take.

If you have exchanged your miles for a certificate, only to find out that you can't actually use it, some airlines will allow you to redeposit the miles back into your frequent flyer account. However, some airlines will charge you a fee for this.

If you find that there are no seats available on a particular date you want to fly, see if you can fly out of another airport nearby. It might be worth driving an extra 50 to 100 miles to catch a free flight from a smaller airport, even if you have to pay for long-term parking.

Most airlines will transfer frequent flyer miles to your heirs upon your death. If there are enough miles for an award, the awards can be issued in their names, and if not then the miles will just be transferred to their accounts.

Once you've collected more than a certain number of miles or flight segments on some airlines, you'll be upgraded to Premier (Silver) or Gold status. These programs let you earn frequent flyer miles more quickly, let you get free or cheap upgrades, and get preferred seating. The mileage levels for status change vary from airline to airline, and the benefits vary as well, but typically one or two overseas flights, or 20,000 to 35,000 U.S. domestic miles will be enough to get you upgraded.

You get benefits on more than just one airline

Many airlines have frequent flyer agreements with other, associated airlines—a good number of them foreign carriers. So, for example, if you book a flight on Taca, a Central American airline, you can actually get credit on American Airlines…if you ask.

The following are the main networks of associated airlines:

- **Oneworld:** Aer Lingus, American Airlines, British Airways, Cathay Pacific, FinnAir, Iberia, LAN Chile, and Qantas.

- **SkyTeam Alliance:** AeroMexico, Air France, Alitalia, Continental, CSA Czech Airlines, KLM, Korean Air, and Northwest.

- **Star Alliance:** Air Canada, Air New Zealand, All Nippon Airways, ANA, Asiana Airlines, Austrian Airlines, British Midland, LOT, Lufthansa Airlines, SAS, Singapore Airlines, Spanair, TAP Portugal, Thai, United Airlines, US Airways, and Varig.

Other ways to collect those miles

Some credit card companies work with frequent flyer programs to provide bonus miles to their customers every time they charge something to their accounts. The plans usually reward their members with one frequent flyer mile for every dollar charged on their credit cards. The following airlines are affiliated with credit cards as shown:

- **Alaska Airlines:** Sea First Bank VISA, CC VISA, or Master Card

- **American Airlines:** Citibank VISA or World Mastercard

- **America West:** Flight Fund

- **Northwest Airlines:** First Bank VISA

- **United Airlines:** First Card VISA

- **US Airways:** Bank of America VISA

American Express also allows you to transfer your loyalty points across into FF programs in the following airlines:

• Continental	• US Airways
• AeroMexico	• Air Canada
• ANA	• El Al Israel
• Global Pass	• Hawaiian Airlines
• JetBlue	• Mexicana

The advantages of frequent flyer programs

- Song
- Southwest
- Virgin Atlantic

You can exchange American Express loyalty points for certificates redeemable at:

- Air France
- Air Jamaica
- Alitalia
- Cathay Pacific
- Frontier
- LAN
- Qantas
- South African Airways
- Swiss
- Virgin Atlantic.

With many credit card companies, you can use your loyalty points to get hotel vouchers as well as FF miles. Therefore, if you were able to save sufficient points with your credit card company, you could eventually "pay" for a trip—flight and accommodation—with saved points alone.

Some telephone companies also provide frequent flyer bonuses for their long-distance customers. Each time you hire a rental car, be sure to inquire about the rental company's affiliation with airline frequent flyer programs. Virtually every company has one, but almost none will award the miles unless you ask about them and specify the airline you want. Most offer a fixed-mileage bonus each time you rent. Additionally, many hotels will offer FF miles when you check in. Again, you'll normally need to ask.

Don't catch the frequent flyer bug

It's often tempting to fly the airline where you have your FF program—even when they cost a bit more. We all know how nice it is to go to the head of the line at check-in, receive upgrades, and get on the plane first. However, you should take stock of what those miles are actually worth.

If a traveler's average domestic redemption to get a free trip is 25,000 miles, then his earned FF miles are worth 1.4 cents each, given that any domestic flight can be bought for under $350 with a little pre-planning. Thus, a 3,000-mile trip earns the traveler $42 worth of FF miles.

If you're paying a premium of more than that just for the sake of flying with the airline that has your FF program, you're losing money; in the long-run, you could effectively buy the award flight cheaper than getting it "free." Now that doesn't make financial sense.

Paying a premium may be worth it to you if you're really driven to reach Platinum Status, but you should keep in mind what it's costing you.

Frequent flyers, frequent renters, and frequent guest awards

A lot of frequent flyers have a dilemma when traveling. They're offered frequent renter awards when booking their car, and frequent guest awards when checking into the hotel. Most of these hotels and rental car companies offer frequent flyer awards as well, and you might wonder which gives you the most value—the air miles or the fidelity points.

Our advice? Stick with the frequent flyer credits anywhere they're available.

Why? Unlike airlines, which normally have fairly competitive rates in a given market, prices on rental cars and hotels vary widely from one market to the next. For example, Hertz may be by far the cheapest when renting in Managua, but up at the high end when renting in New York. In fact, the difference can be so vast from city to city that there's no way that it's worth paying the premium just to rent from the company in order to earn points. The same goes for hotels.

Chapter 8

Hotel and car rentals

Getting a good deal on hotels

All of the major travel sites and most airline sites offer hotel bookings as well, allowing you to book the hotel (and car) when you book the flight. This is quite convenient and you'll be able to find the reservations all in one place. Sometimes there are even special deals available when combining these bookings that are hard to find otherwise.

If you're just looking for a hotel however, head straight over to **Hotels.com**. It's convenient, easy to use, and has excellent worldwide coverage. We recently heard of a special weekend rate in Buenos Aires of $95. When we called by phone to make a booking, we were told that the rate was $175, after which we went into an Internet café in Montevideo and booked the room on Hotels.com for just $89. At times, even the staff at the hotel won't believe the rates you come in with, but we've always found them to be honored.

But don't stop there. Another great hotel site is **TravelWeb**. Formed by a group of large hotel chains, they offer good rates at hundreds of cities around the world. Check them out at *www.travelweb.com*.

Also, it pays to let **SideStep** pop up to cross-check your prices. Recently, Sidestep found a rate at the Hampton Inn in Guayaquil, Ecuador of $45...the rate at the front desk and on Travelocity was over $120.

In addition to SideStep, another handy comparison shopper for hotels is **Travelaxe.com**, a search engine which also works with a small download. They focus on hotel reservations, and can check over 20 hotel-oriented websites for the best prices. Regardless of how you found your hotel rate, it will pay to let Travelaxe compare prices for you.

One thing to remember is that there are virtually ALWAYS discounts available at hotels when they're not full, since most realize that a discounted room is better than an empty one. What you need to do is ask. Admittedly, if you're dragging four suitcases in from the pouring rain you'll not be in a good position to bargain, but even then it's worth a try. If you can, offer them an "out," informing them of your status as a writer on assignment, a veteran, or a member of the AAA or NRA. Sometimes large corporations have discount rates.

And don't forget the rental car

Many rental car bookings are made by answering "Yes" to the car question after making flight or hotel reservations. As we said, it's convenient. The best deals however, are found by starting over, looking for the car from scratch, using the various travel sites.

Unlike hotels, we haven't had much luck asking booking agents for discounts on rental cars, but there are other pointers to remember.

Usually, it's best to ask for the least expensive car available, and if they offer a really good deal on an upgrade, it may pay to take it. Here's where there's some room to manoeuvre. On a recent stop in Managua, an agent offered an upgrade for an extra $50 per week. A few minutes after being told that the previously reserved car was fine, he lowered the upgrade price to $20 per week, which was accepted. When walking outside to pick up the car, it turned out that the upgraded vehicle had previously been brought over from their offsite lot...so they were motivated to have the upgrade accepted. In New York last month, we found that every single car on the lot was the same "intermediate" car. Those who booked intermediates paid for them, but those who booked economy and refused the upgrade offer, got an intermediate at the economy price.

If you're Internet shopping for rental cars, make sure you check to see if the "add-on" costs are included, especially if you need insurance. Some overseas locations even have mandatory insurance options that are not included in the quoted price. The answer here is to read the fine print. In Buenos Aires we recently identified a company that had the lowest quoted price, more than $40 per week less than Hertz. However, after reading the fine print and adding up all the additional costs, Hertz came out $20 per week cheaper...a $60 difference in "extras."

With respect to insurance, many credit card companies will cover rental cars you rent using their card for payment, even overseas. Before you leave, however, call your credit card company and ask specifically what's covered. That way you can waive the insurance when you rent, or only buy what you really need. It's also worth a call to your auto insurance company in the U.S. to check its coverage. They often cover rentals in some form, and will sometimes cover you overseas.

Finally, don't forget those frequent flyer miles. There's often a 500-mile award for booking your rental, as long as you inquire about it.

Chapter 9

Tips from the street-smart traveler

When it's all said and done, there's nothing better than some first-hand experience when looking for the best travel deals. Here are a few tricks that I've come across over the years that I try to keep in mind when traveling.

1. **Ask for a better deal.** This is one approach that can never hurt. Some time ago, I called US Airways at the last minute to book a flight from Groton, Connecticut, to Philadelphia. When quoted a price of $595 (the normal full fare), I thanked the agent and told her that it looked like Amtrak was a better option for this trip. With that, she told me there was a special available for just $240. This works well in hotels, too.

2. **Try a "walk-in."** I've had good luck with both hotels and rental cars with a "walk-in" approach, where I enter the premises and ask what the rates are that day. I tried this at the Balmoral Hotel in Montevideo, Uruguay, just a few weeks ago and was quoted $45 for a room overlooking the park that was posted on their sign at $80. At Snappy Car Rental, I walked in and was quoted a rate less than the one I'd booked in advance, so I took the new one and then canceled the old one.

3. **Recheck your bookings prior to departure.** If you haven't pre-paid the booking, re-check the price prior to departure. I recently saved over $100 on a 10-day car rental by re-checking the price and finding it lower than when I'd reserved it. Again, I booked the new one and canceled the old.

4. **Beware of the overnight stay.** Back in March I found a remarkable $436 promotional airfare from New York to Tokyo. Unfortunately, the arrival of my flight from Ecuador required an overnight stay in New York. The trip ended up costing more, and was less convenient. When striving for the airfare bargain, it's sometimes easy to miss other incidentals adding up, like an extra day in the hotel or with a rental car. You should also factor these in when calculating the value of booking with your frequent flyer airline.

5. **Spend your miles on expensive trips, and earn them on the cheap ones.** I like to earn my miles on the $400 discount flights to New York, and redeem them on $1,000 flights to Phoenix.

6. **Try booking separate flights.** Last year I saved over $300 by booking separate flights on a trip to Miami, Nassau, and Los Angeles rather than booking a single trip...and both prices were from the same airline. On another trip, I saved almost $400 by taking American to Los Angeles and then Southwest Airlines to Phoenix, rather than flying American directly to Phoenix...but be careful of this one if you've got checked baggage or close connections.

7. **When in doubt, enroll in everything.** I never take a flight anymore without being enrolled in the airline's frequent flyer program. Every time I've declined to enroll because I don't normally fly that airline, I've come to regret it on subsequent flights. It's free, and can only help you in the future.

8. **Look early and keep looking.** I've seen fares that go up and down dramatically over the course of a month, and also fares that were only available for a matter of hours. If you've got the time, look for your airfares, cars, and hotels early, and keep an eye on them until you have to buy, or until you see what you know to be a good price. I once noticed a trend where a certain airline lowered its fare to Quito, Ecuador, on the first of every month, then raised it when those limited seats were sold out. It pays to keep an eye on your frequent destinations.

9. **Buy quickly when you know you've got a good price.** Already this year, I lost $200 on a Southwest Airlines flight, and $150 on an American flight, because I waited to "think about it." With the American flight, I missed out just by waiting until after lunch. Know what a good price is for your destination, and move quickly when you see it.

10. **Beware of those who are advertising discounts.** Everyone has seen ads offering 20%, 30%, or 50% savings on airline tickets. Keep in mind that these percentages are normally with respect to the full coach fare, which almost nobody pays. At times I've gotten 50% off the coach fare just by booking a month in advance. Always check these claims by doing some Internet comparison shopping to see what you're really saving.

11. **Run for the phones.** This applies when you've just had a flight canceled or delayed while waiting at the airport. The last place you want to be at that time is in line at the desk with the other 200 passengers on your flight, competing for the 10 available seats on the next flight out. When your flight is canceled, grab your cell phone or head to the nearest phone bank, and make your new booking there. I've often found myself happily on my way while 50% of the line at the counter was still grumbling and waiting for their meal tickets.

   To help with this, I keep the toll-free number (or FF preferred number) for my most frequently used airlines programmed into my cell phone. I also travel with a pocket card which has the number of every airline whose FF program I belong to, along with my frequent flyer number.

12. **Try your own "bait and switch."** Once I've purchased a bargain fare to fly overseas, I sometimes find myself wishing that I had a more convenient flight, since the bargains are often offered at weird hours or days. While I've never gotten one changed in the U.S., I've had luck on two occasions changing to a good flight at the overseas end of the trip, where the agent was happy to put me

on the flight that I was told was "sold out" at my rate in the U.S.

See what works for you

Even though the neighborhood travel agent may no longer be routinely toiling on your behalf, you can still get a good deal without spending too much of your valuable time. See what works for you, and follow your own method each time you travel...it will get easier each time to find the best rates.

Chapter 10

Cover all eventualities

The best way to prepare for all eventualities, and to cover yourself as much as possible, is to learn from the experience of those who've gone before you. Take stock of practical advice, and prepare and plan your journey with a cool head, before you travel. That way you'll be better able to deal with problems that may arise, and you'll be far less likely to find yourself in a situation that you don't know how to deal with.

Effective preparation and planning are significant components of any positive travel experience. You can make yourself appear and feel less vulnerable, and more at ease in any strange place, by feeling that you have a safe element of control over the situation. The opposite is true if you are suddenly plunged into an unfamiliar and inhospitable-looking environment, when you've done none of the basic groundwork that would help you to get your bearings.

Think ahead. Ask questions, and find out the answers. Don't let others profit from your vulnerability.

Beware unsolicited travel opportunities, and telemarketing fraud

Sometimes, where a deal seems too good to be true, it might turn out to have hidden charges. For example, many free vacations or special giveaway offers will require you to stay at a specific hotel that charges exorbitant rates. Beware of extremely low-priced offers, unsolicited offers involving Florida or Hawaii, and opportunities where you're being pressured into buying on the spot.

Always ask detailed questions (e.g., what is covered by the price and what isn't; whether there are any additional charges; the names of the hotels, airlines, airports, and restaurants; exact dates and times; cancelation policies; and refund policies), and **get it all in writing before you buy.**

You should never give out personal information like credit card numbers, social security numbers, and bank account numbers, to an unsolicited telephone salesperson. Nor should you ever give out your frequent flyer number over the phone, unless you've initiated the call.

What you can do to protect yourself from fraud

When all is as it should be, there should be no problem in asking a telemarketer for a company telephone number, and calling back the next day, after you've had time to check the situation out. You can call the Better Business Bureau in your area and use the company's phone number to verify that it is in fact a legitimate business. You can also ascertain whether there have been any complaints against it. Find out about the company in question through the state attorney general's office, or through your local consumer protection agency, which you can locate through the website: *www.consumeraffairs.com.*

You'll do a lot to protect yourself from fraud by always paying with a credit card—never with a check, cash, or money order. When you pay for purchases with a credit card, you are automatically covered by the Fair Credit Billing Act against fraudulent charges.

Just because a company has an impressive, colorful newspaper ad, and a toll-free 800 number (remember: it's possible for any individual to get his or her very own 800 number), doesn't mean it's safe, or indeed reliable. Unfortunately, as the process goes, time must elapse before a company will generate enough complaints for the Federal Trade Commission to start an investigation.

Watch out for airport scams

At the airport, do not give your tickets to anyone other than an agent of the airline at the ticketing/check-in counter, the gate, or the airline's offices. One scam involves a criminal dressing up in a uniform similar to that of the airline, and approaching people in the airport with some excuse for checking (taking) their tickets. If in doubt, ask to see an airline ID, and remember that genuine staff-members, who have nothing to hide, and who are there to help you with your needs, won't take umbrage at being asked for their company credentials. Any problems you encounter should be reported to the **National Fraud Information Center** (the hotline is *800-876-7060*), and to security personnel at the airport in question.

While you're passing through the airport, if you have more bags than you can comfortably manage, you should take the extra couple of minutes to get a baggage cart—otherwise you will be distracted from what's going on around you, because you're too busy struggling to juggle your load. If you get distracted by these difficulties, you won't be as vigilant as necessary when it comes to keeping an eye on the bags that matter most. Criminals target travelers who look harried or distressed; they can spot them a mile off. A common ploy is for a scam artist to bump into you, scattering your bags, and while this person helps you to gather up your belongings, an accomplice is walking away with one of your bags—and these people have a knack of knowing which bags contain the most valuable items.

Get country-specific information

The U.S. State Department issues advice for travelers, which includes country-specific warnings, and **consular information sheets** for every country. It is in your best interests to familiarize yourself with this information before you travel. To be forewarned is to be forearmed—if you're wise you'll make yourself aware of any recent dangerous circumstances, such as political and social unrest, in your place of destination.

Each country's consular information sheet also lists the location of the local U.S. embassy or consulate, and gives details of specific immigration practices and procedures, local health conditions, unusual currency regulations, crime and security information, punitive laws, and drug penalties which vary greatly from country to country. You can access this information at the *website: ftp.stolaf.edu:/pub/travel-advisories/advisories,* and you can subscribe to receive regular electronic updates on your destination by emailing: *travel-advisories-request@stolaf.edu.*

Country-specific info—South East Asia's punitive laws

Thailand: Thailand's military-style police force frequently raids bars and nightclubs in order to root out underage drinkers and recreational drug-users. During these raids the police usually inspect the ID of every person on the premises, and force everyone (foreigners included) to provide a urine sample for an on-the-spot drugs test. Possession of drugs (even without the intent to distribute) will bring hefty penalties—usually a prison sentence that's anything up to life behind bars.

Drug trafficking is a capital crime; offenders are sentenced to death by shooting.

Singapore: Singapore adopts a zero tolerance approach to drug abuse. There is a mandatory death sentence for anyone found to be trafficking in drugs, and more than 30 people have been hanged since the law came into effect in 1975.

For those caught abusing illegal substances, repeat offenders face mandatory sentences of seven to 13 years in prison, plus caning (with a six-foot rotan soaked in brine, carried out by a martial arts expert). A first offence for use of Ecstasy carries a 12- to 18-month sentence.

Serious acts of vandalism, as well as some immigration offences are punishable by mandatory caning.

Littering is seen as a less serious act of vandalism, punishable by public service; if you visit the city you will notice people in yellow, high-visibility vests, with "Corrective Work Order" stamped on their backs, who spend hours picking up litter (in Singapore that amounts to matches and cigarette butts). These people are convicted litterbugs serving out their punishment; they also pay fines, and must receive state-sponsored counselling. You'll notice they often cover their faces with scarves to conceal their identities.

It is illegal to sell or possess chewing gum in Singapore. Spitting on the ground, jaywalking, and failing to flush a public toilet are all punishable offences that were introduced to foster harmony between the country's three divergent, and equally weighted cultures—Singaporean, Chinese, and Indian.

Malaysia: This country also takes a draconian approach to drug trafficking—it's a capital offence, punishable by hanging. This is how they see it: Malaysia is not a drug-producing country and shouldn't have to endure the corrupting influence, and related problems, of Western vices. The government sees the death penalty as a major step toward its ideal of a utopian society.

The rotan is also in common usage in Malaysia.

Indonesia: Persons found to be in possession of narcotics for personal use, receive a 10-year prison sentence (and Indonesian prisons are notoriously squalid and dangerous), traffickers incur a 15-year sentence, and manufacturers of illegal substances are executed by a firing squad.

Be sure to buy the necessary plug adaptor before you leave the U.S., otherwise you'll find that it's difficult to find the one you need—the locals at your destination don't have much call for adaptors that will enable them to use U.S. appliances.

If you are going on a long-haul trip, or indeed moving oversees, it is a good idea to arrange to talk directly to the representative in the State Department who is responsible for dealing with that country. She or he most likely will have been there, and will be equipped with extensive, up-to-date knowledge of the place, the political and social climate, and have a cache of priceless anecdotal advice to share with you, which is difficult to come by in print material.

Useful numbers

For information or assistance contact:

- **U.S. Department of State**, *tel. 202-647-4000, 202-647-5225,* or (toll-free) *800-877-8339*

  — **Hotline for American Travelers**, *tel. 202-647-5225*

  — **Citizens Consular Services**, *tel. 202-647-3444*

  — **Passport Services**, *tel. 202-647-0518*

  — **Visa Services**, *tel. 202-663-1225*

Where taking a photograph could land you in trouble

Snap-happy tourists take note: In some African countries, it is an offence to take a photograph of an official person or building. In Kenya, for example, it is forbidden to photograph the national flag, the President, soldiers, uniformed policemen, official buildings, prisons, convicts, and military barracks.

In Tanzania, individuals have been detained and/or had their cameras and film confiscated for taking pictures of hospitals, schools, bridges, industrial sites, and airports.

Installations that are prohibited from being photographed are not always marked. If in doubt, check with a local person before taking a picture (taken from *Secrets of the Untourist*, published by *International Living*).

- **U.S. Department of Transport Travel Advisory,** *tel.* (toll-free) *800-221-0673*

- **Center for Disease Control,** *tel. 404-332-4559; fax: 404-639-3311*

Airplane safety

Fatal accidents involving airplanes are relatively very rare—still. In fact, the chances of getting killed in a plane crash are less that one in a million, which means that using commercial flights is still one the safest ways to travel. Of course there will always be risks, and there are some things that you can do to increase your chances of survival in the event of a crash. Although opinions on this subject differ, it is thought that sitting close to the wings is the safest place to be, as the airplane structure is most reinforced here.

In the event of a fire, natural-fiber clothes such as wool, cotton, and silk will offer you greater protection than synthetic garments, which are likely to melt or ignite, produce black smoke and toxic fumes, and cause serious burns.

Bear in mind when you board a plane, that in the event of a fire, the cabin will quickly fill with dark smoke. It is a good idea, therefore, to count the rows of seats from your own seat to the nearest exit (both ahead and behind), so that, should you be required to, you will be able to navigate your escape route by touch alone.

Stiletto (or similar) heels should not be worn on a flight; they can snag on the escape slide, impede your escape, and further endanger you and the other passengers.

If you are traveling with a baby you should bring your own aircraft-approved infant safety seat, and it should have been made *after* 1985.

The flight attendant will draw your attention to the location of your personal flotation device during the safety demonstration. It most likely will be an inflatable life vest in a plastic bag stored beneath your seat (occasionally in your armrest), or it might be your actual seat cushion. If you notice any problems with your flotation device, inform the flight attendant before take-off.

You should also forewarn your flight attendant if you have any serious medical conditions or disabilities for which you might require assistance, and if you're flying unaccompanied, you should point him/her to the location of your emergency medications, such as those for angina, epilepsy, or anaphylactic shock.

Know the risks of DVT

Deep vein thrombosis (DVT) is a potentially life-threatening condition that has been closely associated with flying of late. It affects mainly the veins in the lower leg and the thigh, and involves the formation of a clot in a large vein, which can interfere with circulation of the area, and can sometimes break away and travel through the blood stream. The danger is that the clot could then lodge in the brain, lungs, or heart, and cause serious complications.

Risks include: prolonged, immobilized sitting on long flights (and bus and car journeys), recent surgery or trauma (especially hip, knee, or gynecological surgery); fractures; childbirth within the past six months, smoking, and the use of some medications such as some estrogen and birth control pills.

The incidence of DVT is more commonly seen in adults over 60, but can occur at any age. Familiarize yourself with the symptoms: pain, tenderness, and/or swelling in **one leg only,** and increased warmth in the affected leg can also cause the skin to become red. There is growing evidence that passengers on flights of more than four hours are at an increased risk of developing DVT.

If you are concerned about potential problems, you should take a proactive approach and buy a pair of special flight socks (widely available from drugstores and pharmacies) before you undertake your journey. These knee-length socks create a graduated compression system that significantly improves the blood flow in the legs, and also helps to relieve discomfort, and reduce the risk of swelling.

There are other measures you can take to stave off circulatory problems: you should get up and walk around the cabin as often as possible. Exercise your calve muscles while you're seated, by flexing your feet (many airlines provide information sheets about DVT, for passengers on long-haul flights, detailing suitable exercises), sit comfortably without crossing your legs, and massage your calves lightly from time to time. Minimize your intake of caffeine, alcohol, and salt (during and prior to your flight), and stay well hydrated by drinking lots of clear fluids. Avoid prolonged contact between the edge of your seat and the backs of your calves—use the footrest if it helps.

Flying for two? Air travel and pregnancy

You'll be glad to know that flying doesn't pose any particular risks to a healthy pregnant woman or her baby.

Obstetricians say that the safest time for a pregnant woman to fly is during the second trimester (18 to 24 weeks) when she usually feels at her best, and is in the least danger of experiencing a miscarriage or premature labor.

Women in the third trimester (25 to 36 weeks) might be required by their doctors to stay within a few miles of home, because of proximity to medical care in case of problems such as hypertension, phlebitis, or false or premature labor.

Domestic travel is usually permitted until 36 weeks, and international travel may be prohibited after 32 weeks.

When making your reservations, it is a good idea to check the airline's policy on pregnant travelers: some will require medical forms to be completed.

In terms of comfort, an aisle seat at the bulkhead will provide the most space, but a seat over the wing (the middle of the plane) will give the smoothest ride. Also, you will probably want a seat quite near the toilets.

Women travelling with infants should keep in mind that babies younger than six weeks old should not fly because their alveoli (little nodes in the lungs) are not completely functional. Infants are particularly susceptible to pain during pressure changes at take-off and landing. Breastfeeding or bottle-feeding during take-off and landing will alleviate the discomfort.

Tips for comfort:

- Take a short walk around the cabin every half-hour during a smooth flight.
- Boost your lower leg circulation (and reduce swelling) by extending the ankles and flexing the feet frequently.
- Always extend the seatbelt and fasten at the pelvic level—rather than above your bump.
- Drink plenty of clear fluid to stay hydrated.

General health safety

Make sure you are up to date with your prescription medicines when you're traveling abroad, and bring a copy of the doctor's script just in case your medication gets mislaid. All medications should be kept in their original packaging or pharmacy tub with a clean legible label—otherwise you could face problems at customs.

It's a good idea to bring your medication with you, on-board a flight, in your hand luggage, in case your luggage should get delayed or lost. Pharmacy laws vary from place to place, but generally speaking, most pharmacists will give you an emergency supply to tide you over, once they can refer to your doctor's written instructions. If you come up against a refusal, try a few more pharmacies before you give up; they're not always in accord about their individual policies.

You should carry a card listing any serious health conditions, the required medication (trade name, generic name, and manufacturer), dosages and frequency, and your doctor's home and work telephone numbers. It is very important to include a list of allergies, and your blood type. If you have a life-threatening condition, it is also recommended that you wear a medic-alert bracelet or necklace at all times—Accident and Emergency-staff the world-over will check for these immediately, and recognize their significance.

Take note of your companion's blood type.

Street safety

There are a number of things that you need to think about in a foreign country that may never occur to you at home.

Be sure to plan the journey from the airport to your hotel before you leave home. Find out which taxis are official/authorized, and roughly how much your journey should cost; the local tourism website should provide this information. Agree on a fare before you get into the taxi. Be careful about who you let help you with your bags.

If you'll be taking a bus, find out the number, and make sure you know how to ask for your stop. If you don't speak the language, write the name of the hotel and street on a piece of paper that you can show to the driver, and then sit near the front of the vehicle so that you won't be forgotten. Similarly, if you're going to travel by train, ascertain the route and the stop, and use a small street-map to get from the station to your hotel. Discreetly take note of who follows you off a train or bus, and if you're in any doubt, just go and sit over a coffee for a while, in the nearest decent-looking bar, restaurant, or hotel.

Carry as little cash as possible for the trip from the airport to your accommodation—just enough for travel, refreshments, and a meal if necessary.

If you drive, and are involved in a minor car accident in a foreign country, you should not leave your car. Instead, you should drive to a well-lit area, such as a shopping mall or hotel, and call the police. Criminals will sometimes follow foreigners from the airport, bump their rental cars in a remote location, and then rob them.

Similarly, if you need directions, ask at the airport information desk before you leave the airport, and once you're on the road you can ask at a hotel, gas station, bank, or restaurant. Try not to draw attention to the fact that you are lost (indeed that you are a lost foreigner), whether you are driving or on foot.

Carry maps and cameras discreetly, and avoid clothing (such as fanny-packs worn above your clothes), and jewelry that readily identify you as a traveler.

Vaccinations

If you are going to a remote or tropical destination, you will need to see your doctor about vaccinations and malaria tablets at least eight weeks before you travel.

Find out the risks and vaccine requirements at your destination through the **Centers for Disease Control**, *tel.* (toll free) *877-FYI-TRIP; fax:* (toll free) *888-232-3299; website:*

www.cdc.gov/travel/vaccinat/html.

You should store valuables, travel documents, passports, extra cash and cards, and a list of emergency telephone and credit/debit card numbers in the hotel safe, located either in a closet in your room or at the main reception.

You should make photocopies of important documents such as driving license, passport, tickets, prescriptions, and insurance policy, before you travel, and keep them separate from the originals, e.g. in a different piece of luggage.

Be aware that crowds, and crowded places everywhere draw pickpockets.

Dos and don'ts if you get arrested abroad

If you are arrested abroad, you should immediately ask the arresting officers to allow you to contact the nearest embassy or consulate

Safety tips for female travelers

Maddening though it is, even in the 21st century, every country and culture has its own views of what it considers "appropriate behavior" for women. The reaction to flouting these expectations can range from quiet disapproval to criminal charges and punishment. Did you know that in Laos it's illegal to invite a Lao citizen of the opposite sex to your hotel room? In Saudi Arabia foreign travelers have been arrested for "improper dress."

When abroad you should make a point of observing how the local women dress, and attempt to blend in as much as possible—try not to wear clothes that will draw unwelcome attention.

Bear in mind that, unfortunately, a smile, a hairstyle, the way you carry yourself, eye contact, and the distance between people when they're talking can have profoundly different interpretations from culture to culture. Watch local women for your cues.

When you're out and about, if you need to carry a purse, loop the strap around your neck and put one arm through, so that the bag is not on the side of you that is exposed to the road. (Bag-snatchers often drive very close to the curb on motorbikes, and grab bags that are within arm's length.) Always carry your purse toward the front of your body, with the flap facing your body. In any open space, don't ever let your purse dangle off of your shoulder or elbow—it's much easier to snatch.

Avoid wearing expensive-looking jewelry—including, or perhaps especially, costume jewelry which is designed to catch the eye. A thief won't know it's fake until after he has robbed, frightened, and hurt you.

representing your country. As a citizen of another country, you have this right. If you are refused or just ignored, continue to ask periodically until they agree to let you contact your embassy or consulate.

Try to stay calm, so that you will avoid doing something that might irritate or provoke the arresting officers.

Do not admit to anything, or volunteer any unnecessary information to the police. Don't sign anything—even if you feel like you're being impolite; decline until such a time as an attorney or representative from your embassy/consulate can examine the material.

Accept no one at face value. Be sure to ask the embassy/consulate representative for some formal identification before discussing your situation with him/her.

Do not be fooled into thinking that helping those who are detaining you, will hasten your release; unfortunately the law doesn't work like that in many countries around the world.

One tip for dealing with unwanted attention
By Donna Garvin

"Last year I spent a few months traveling around SE Asia with my sister Ger. We found that in some of the less-trammeled places we visited, we were something of a curiosity to the local guys, which resulted in some unwanted attention at times. We were happy to talk to them, and to socialize together but sometimes local men were very persistent, and seemed to see all women as weak-willed or coy. Neither of us wanted to resort being rude, and my sister had a trick that she used to great affect. Before we went traveling, she had a photograph taken of herself with her friend's husband and toddler, looking like quite the happy little family. When she flashed this photo to the local guys, their attitudes changed immediately and perceptibly, in accord with her new "status." We found that Asian men have a high degree of respect for the family (the same is true of Middle Eastern men), and this respect was extended towards my sister, once they thought she was married, and a mother. They treated her more like a sister after that. They didn't question or even notice the fact that she wasn't wearing a ring—presumably because it would have been impolite to mention it. Clever indeed..."

You should contact the consulate or your embassy for protection and assistance in getting out of the country once you are released.

Travel safety checklist—photocopy and use:

Item	Details	Tick b
Travel and health documents	Insurance certificate.	☐
	Drivers license.	☐
	Passport.	☐
	Prescriptions and generic names.	☐
	Card detailing allergies, illnesses, and blood type.	☐
	Reservation and confirmation numbers for flights and hotels.	☐
	Credit/debit card numbers.	☐
	List of emergency U.S. phone numbers and local embassy/consulate numbers.	☐
(None of the above should be packed in your checked luggage.)		
Photocopies of documents	Keep separate from the originals.	☐
Medic-alert necklace/bracelet	To be worn at all times.	☐
Prescription medications	Still in the packaging in which you received them, with original labels. (Carry these onto the plane.)	☐
Plug adapter	Buy this before you go away.	☐
Insect repellent	Preferably containing DEET (although there are associated concerns, and it is believed to be unsuitable for young children). You can look into buying a plug-in mosquito repellent once you arrive.	☐
First aid & medications	Painkillers (with anti-inflammatory action where suitable), anti-diarrhoea pills, mild laxatives, sachets of rehydration salts, support bandage, bandaids, antihistamine pills, antacids, motion sickness pills, antihistamine cream, hydrocortisone cream (for itchy bites and rashes), burns spray and dressing, styptic powder, antiseptic cream, small plastic bottle of saline solution (can be used as an eyewash or to irrigate a wound), sterile dressings, adhesive tape, coldsore cream, tweezers, safety pins, small scissors (store in your checked luggage)	☐
Water-sterilization tablets for exotic locations	Potassium permanganate or similar.	☐
Spare glasses/contacts	Don't forget the contact solutions.	☐
Sun protection cream	Preferably waterproof, long lasting, and with SPF 15 or higher. It's worthwhile packing aloe vera gel or aftersun lotion.	☐
Freezer bags	For dirty clothes and shoes.	☐
Hard candy	For cabin pressurization. To be kept in your hand luggage, or on your person.	☐

Appendix A

Online travel resources

Here is just a sampling of the Internet travel resources available. Each of the travel services below offers information on airfares, cars, and hotels. Those websites which don't actually make the booking themselves, connect you automatically to the website that does.

- **Bestfares:** This Quickfare Finder covers all of North America, the Caribbean, and Central and South America. Europe is being added at this time. It also has a lot of useful travel info on the site, like ATM locations and currency converters. Bestfares.com is an information source and does not issue airline tickets online. *Website: www.bestfares.com.*

- **Expedia:** Its Expert Searching and Pricing (ESP) technology delivers comprehensive flight options and allows customers to dynamically build complete trips that combine flights. Expedia is the fourth-largest travel agency in the U.S. *Website: www.expedia.com.*

- **Hotels.com:** Reportedly the Internet's largest specialized booking service for discount accommodation worldwide. It's got excellent info that you can use to compare hotels. We've found these prices to be nearly always the best.

- **Orbitz:** Originally started when five airlines—American, Continental, Northwest, and United—came together to develop one of the first travel websites. It now has 455 airlines in its inventory, as well as 45,000 hotel properties, and 23 rental car affiliations. Good customer service. *Website: www.orbitz.com.*

- **Priceline:** Offers travel planning services plus a unique "name your own price" feature, where you can name the price you're willing to pay for a ticket. If an airline accepts your "bid," the ticket is purchased. The prices are excellent, but you don't get to review the itinerary until the purchase is final. If you can be flexible, this is a good option. Beware though, that some additional fees will be added to your bid—up to $114 for an international flight—so make sure you take that into consideration when you set your bid price. All Priceline flights must originate in the U.S. *Website: www.priceline.com.*

- **Sherman's Travel:** Claiming to be your "unbiased" guide to the best travel deals, it assembles a good report of current travel deals from many different sources. It also has a free newsletter with the week's 25 best travel bargains. *Website: www.shermanstravel.com.*

- **Sidestep:** Offers airfares, hotels, and cars. This service pops up when it "sees" you entering dates on a travel site. *Website: www.sidestep.com.*

- **Travelaxe:** Focused on hotel bookings, this service also works by checking over 20 hotel-related websites and by allowing you to compare prices. *Website: www.travelaxe.com.*

- **Travelocity:** Born of travel innovator Sabre (the world's largest travel agent reservation system), it's been a pioneer in web-based reservations. Offers 24-hour support and a good "flexible dates" search tool. *Website: www.travelocity.com.*

- **TravelWeb:** A great hotel site formed by a consortium of large hoteliers. It offers good prices on hundreds of cities around the world. *Website: www.travelweb.com.*

- **Travelzoo:** Travelzoo claims to be the Internet's largest publisher of sales and specials, available directly from hundreds of other travel companies. It has over six million subscribers. *Website: www.travelzoo.com.*

Appendix B

International and domestic airlines

Here's a partial list of some reliable U.S. and domestic airlines, along with their contact information.

- **Aer Lingus,** via Dublin, Ireland: the U.S., UK, the Netherlands, Denmark, Germany, Belgium, Switzerland, Italy, France, and Spain; *tel. (800)223-6537; website: www.aerlingus.com.*

- **Aerolineas Argentinas,** via Argentina: South America; *tel. (800)333-0276; website: www.aeroargentinas.com.*

- **Air Canada,** from Canada and the U.S. to Europe and Asia; *tel. (888)247-2262; website:www.aircanada.com.* Air Canada's economy airline, Tango, may offer lower fares but they are only available through its website at *www.flytango.com* or its reservations center at *tel. (800)315-1390.*

- **Air France,** via France: Africa, China, Madagascar, Israel, Australia, Thailand, Indonesia, Mexico, South America, England, Germany, Austria, Italy, Finland, Canada, Hong Kong, Iran, Pakistan, the Commonwealth of Independent States or CIS (the countries of the former Soviet Union), Caribbean, Eastern Europe; *tel. (800)237-2747; website: www.airfrance.com/us.*

- **Air New Zealand,** Australia, New Zealand, Fiji, Samoa, Tonga, Indonesia, Singapore, Hong Kong, Japan, Taiwan, England, and Germany; *tel.* (800)262-1234; *website: www.airnz.co.nz.*

- **ALIA Royal Jordanian Airlines,** Middle East, Central and Eastern Europe, Greece, Canada, Pakistan, India, Singapore, and Thailand; *tel.* (800)223-0470; *website: www.rja.com.jo.*

- **Alitalia Airlines,** via Italy: Western Europe, Russia, Ukraine, Japan, Africa, Australia, and Canada; *tel.* (800)223-5730; *website: www.alitaliausa.com* and *www.alitalia.com.*

- **American Airlines,** the U.S., Japan, Europe, and South America; tel. (800)433-300; *website: www.aa.com.*

- **American TransAir,** Mexico, the Caribbean, Venezuela, England, France, and Germany; *tel.* (800)225-2995; *website: www.ata.com.*

- **America West,** based out of Phoenix, Arizona: flies to the West Coast, Midwest, East Coast, New York, Washington, and Western Canada; *tel.* (800)235-9292; *website: www.americawest.com.*

- **Austrian Airlines,** Western Europe, the Middle East, Africa, Asia; *tel.* (800)843-0002; *website:www.austrianair.com.*

- **British Airways,** via London, England: Western Europe, Asia, Africa, Australia, New Zealand, the Caribbean, the Middle East, South America, Canada; *tel.* (800)247-9297; *website: www.britishairways.com.*

- **Cheap Flights,** U.S., Canada, Australia, Hong Kong, South Africa, Denmark, France, Germany, Spain, UK, and Ireland; *website: www.cheapflights.com.*

- **Continental Airlines,** Australia, Japan, Mexico, Ecuador, Europe, Canada, the U.S., the Caribbean, and Indonesia; *tel.* (800)231-0856;*website: www.continental.com.*

- **Copa Airlines,** from the U.S. to Columbia, Argentina, Mexico, Venezuela, Guatemala, Ecuador, Cuba, Jamaica, Peru, Nicaragua, Panama, Haiti, Costa Rica, Puerto Rico, El Salvador, Chile, Dominican Republic, and Brazil; *tel.* (800)FLY-COPA; *website: www.copaair.com.*

- **Easy Jet,** the UK, Portugal, Spain, France, Netherlands, Denmark, Germany, Switzerland, Czechoslovakia, and Greece; *website: www.easyjet.com.*

- **FinnAir,** via Helsinki: Western Europe, the Far East, and Russia; *tel. (800)950-5000; website: www.finnair.com.*

- **Garuda Indonesia,** via Indonesia: Asia, Australia, and Hawaii; *tel. (800)342-7832; website: www.garuda-indonesia.com.*

- **IcelandAir,** via Iceland: Scotland, England, Scandinavia, and Luxembourg; *tel. (800)223-5500; website: www.icelandair.com.*

- **KLM Royal Dutch Airlines,** via the Netherlands: Eastern Europe, Western Europe, the Caribbean, Canada, Africa, Asia, and the Middle East; *tel. (800)777-5553; website: www.klm.com.*

- **LAN Chile Airlines,** Chile, Argentina, Uruguay, Australia, Tahiti, Peru, Venezuela, Brazil, Spain, and Germany; *tel. (800)735-5526; website: www.lanchile.com.*

- **Lufthansa Airlines,** via Germany: the Middle East, Asia, Africa, Scandinavia, Western Europe, Canada, and the Caribbean; *tel. (800)645-3880; website: www.lufthansa.com.*

- **Midwest Airlines,** the Midwest, Northeast, California, and Florida in the U.S.; *tel. (800)452-2022; website: www.midwestairlines.com.*

- **North American Airlines,** charters, leases, and vacations to California, Florida, and the Caribbean; *tel. (718)656-2650; website: www.northamair.com.*

- **Northwest Airlines,** England, Germany, Scotland, Thailand, Philippines, Singapore, Asia, the U.S., Australia, the Caribbean, and Canada; *tel. (800)447-4747; website: www.nwa.com.*

- **Qantas,** Australia, New Zealand, Fiji, Asia, Germany, Italy, England, South Africa, and Zimbabwe; *tel. (800)227-4500; website: www.qantas.com.*

- **Ryanair,** Ireland, the UK, Spain, France, Belgium, Norway, Sweden, Denmark, Germany, Switzerland, Italy; *website: www.ryanair.com.*

- **SAS,** via Scandinavia: Western Europe, Poland, Hungary, Turkey, Russia, Israel, Greece, Singapore, Japan, Thailand, and China; *tel. (800)221-2350; website: www.scandinavian.net.*

- **Southwest,** East and West coasts and the southwest U.S.; *tel. (800)435-9792; website: www.southwest.com.*

- **Taca,** flies from the U.S. to Central and South America; *tel. (800)535-8780; website: www.taca.com.*

- **TAP** Air Portugal, via Portugal: Greece, South America, Africa, and Western Europe; *tel. (800)221-7370; website: www.tap-airportugal.us.*

- **US Airways,** England, the U.S., Germany, France, Bermuda, the Bahamas, and Canada; *tel. (800)428-4322; website: www.usairways.com.*

- **United Airlines,** Asia, South America, the U.S., Central America, and Western Europe; *tel. (800)241-6522; website: www.united.com.*

- **Varig,** Europe, South America, Central America, the Caribbean, Asia, and Africa; *tel. (800)GO-VARIG; website: www.varig.com.*

- **Virgin Atlantic,** Europe, the UK, South America, Central America, the Caribbean, Asia, India, and Africa; *tel. (800)821-5438; website: www.virgin-atlantic.com/en/us.*